THE UNSEEN WORLD

THE UNSEEN WORLD

DAVID ELKINS

Cover design by Doowah Design.
Cover illustration by Tilke Elkins.
Photo of David Elkins by Denise Bernier.

This book was printed on Ancient Forest Friendly paper.
Printed and bound in Canada by Hignell Book Printing.

We acknowledge the support of The Canada Council for the Arts and the Manitoba Arts Council for our publishing program.

Library and Archives Canada Cataloguing in Publication

Elkins, David, author
The unseen world / David Elkins.

Poems.
ISBN 978-1-927426-05-0 (pbk.)

I. Title.

PS8609.L535U58 2013 C811'.6 C2013-902853-6

Signature Editions
P.O. Box 206, RPO Corydon, Winnipeg, Manitoba, R3M 3S7
www.signature-editions.com

To Valmai,
Tilke
Rupert
Thomas Wolfe
&
Timothy

CONTENTS

IV

GUARDIAN OF CHILDREN, MAKER OF MUSIC

V

NOTHING STAYS THE SAME

VI

FORESTS OF THE HEART

Why *The Unseen World?*

Among the first poems to inspire me were those by Blake, Gerard Manley Hopkins, Rilke, Emily Dickinson and others whose work evoked the sense of a world beyond the senses. How did they conjure these complex emotions with such simple words? Did they set out to write this way or did the poems just come to them "out of the ether"? Were they from a different race entirely?

My wife recently gave me a remarkable book called *Super Brain* by Rudolph "Rudy" E. Tanzi, a professor of neurology at Harvard, an expert on the physical brain, and Deepak Chopra, with his focus on the spiritual side of the mind-body connection. It's a worthy collaboration. Tanzi describes the breakthroughs made in the last decade in understanding how the brain works, particularly its astonishing ability to regenerate and rewire its circuitry. Chopra draws connections to a creative universal consciousness with its emphasis on delight.

In the end, both writers arrive at the same place by quite different paths. Despite the brain's wonders, Tanzi concludes, "We must never forget that the true seat of human existence is in the mind. To which the brain bows like the most devoted and intimate of servants."

Many of the poems in *The Unseen World* attempt to link the physical world of the senses to an overreaching consciousness and to answer the question "Who am I?" with a simple "I am."

David Elkins
Montreal, 2013

I

TABERNACLE OF EARTH

Come forth into the light of things, let nature be your teacher.

— William Wordsworth

I thank God for this most amazing day, for the leaping greenly spirits of trees, and for the blue dream of sky and for everything which is natural, which is infinite, which is yes.

— e.e. cummings

Magic

Cry of king quail
encircles the bright air,
juniper and prickly pear.
even stones and colored sand,
share in this undivided joy.

Grunt of *javelina*
domes the whole night sky.
Emboldened shadows
sent by moon and stars
dance among our secret selves.

Loons

A loon dives,
shivers the still lake,
glides into another world
where his mate already swims,
weightless, focused
on what might pass for memory.
her bright garnet eyes
see what we can no longer see.

All night I lie beside you
in a forest of swaying weeds,
sharp-finned fish nip at my skin,
I know I won't die from their bites
but just the same...
A liquid moon floats above the alders,
a golden-hulled rescue ship
sailing off the edge of the world.

The birds are submerged so long
I hold my own breath for their safety,
at last they resurface
in a way that makes everything else
unimportant.

Red tulip

Red tulip
lights up this small white room
with green and crimson fireworks,
O ceaseless flower,
O unconsidered time,
Leaf blossom root
Sing loud.

Three lindens

Three lindens grow by a green river
through short hot summers,
wind entreats leaves to befriend one another,
The river, always new,
steams in the cool morning,
pays no attention to the stories
banks whisper
of the dangerous sea.

Three churches stand nearby
empty of what is sacred,
tabernacle of earth,
catechism of tree,
chalice of water,
sea no more to be feared than eternity.

Tipsy moon

An old Chinese poet wondered
what is better, poetry or wine?

After the office party
I walk out to the tangled orchard
(Not a single branch pruned all summer)
Amid sweet fruit,
a smirking silver moon rises on the tips of a pear tree,
a first autumn breeze ruffles golden leaves.

Duck eggs

She lays eleven mottled brown eggs
under a bush in the busy park,
her mate lays one black sideways eye on them,
cocks his iridescent head and flies off north.

They hatch
one moonless night,
she tumbles off-springs
into stone-rimmed pond,
too young to fly
they paddle close
she will not leave them.

Brindled like them,
she waits and watches,
keeps dangerous gulls at bay,
counts them with her orange beak,

I count them too
and think of poems I've made
and keep locked away in a drawer.

Closing up

Every winter chipmunks
overrun the summer house,
in spring we find sharp
husks of butternuts
tucked into pillowcases
secreted under sheets.
Stale smells that need
June windows open for a day

September now,
My wife and I agree
we want them gone.

This morning
as we drink our coffee,
one sits atop a fence post,
munches a fat green nut,
her honey coat
catches the early sun,
she turns breakfast
in tiny hands
and makes the yellow fruit
look tasty as bacon

We have no stomach
for poison and killer traps,
Then recall,
five days before,
a red-tailed hawk
stood on that very post.

ramrod straight,
swivel of tawny head,
left, right, up, down,
grip of claw,
hook of beak,
black eyes,
missed nothing.

Winter preparations

Dusty mountain road
rimmed with golden chamisa,
it's held its colour into December.

Nothing to think but sky,
Nothing to desire but clouds,
Nothing to do but empty the heart.

II

DROWNED IN EVERY KIND OF LOVE

Physical pleasure is a sensual experience no different from pure seeing
or the pure sensation with which a fine fruit fills the tongue;
it is a great unending experience, which is given us, a knowing...

— Rainer Maria Rilke

...when wish is merest touch I bend
like her whose curve is heaven over earth
and love beneath me far and far
makes of my flesh a miracle of stars

— Gwendolyn MacEwen

Moon

Sometimes I look at the moon,
sometimes not,
moon cares not

Call love a daytime sky
or a night sky
heart doesn't care

Night never cries for stars
or mornings weep for moon

We look out through curtains
scarcely moved by a tendril of night wind
see the moon caught up in leaves
and tremble.

Night beach

Pale branches beat in shore pines,
a girl you hardly know abandons her clothes
dons the garment of light.
You enter the bright caress of surf
breathe in the fragrance
of a body not your own.

The sea swells silver
roughened by wings of air,
we become angels
drowned in every kind of love.

Wind

The blurred eyes of the moon
look down through sycamore.
You taught me to love the dark,
I reach out to touch your face
almost forgetting you are gone.

Partings

We are not lovers now
or hope to be,
meet at expensive restaurants
where you say you'll pay.

I gaze down
at the heavy silverware,
your pale hands,
you believe so much
I believe so little
I can't see the totemic animals
you say are hiding in your eyes.

Wine goes undrunk
Flesh untasted
Our plates fill up with pain
And are cleared away again.

At the end of Agua Fria Street
Our Lady of Guadalupe
welcomes us with a raised hand,
a bit of plaster worked to look like flesh.
When I turn at last to look at you
you say you are drenched in roses
And yes, I believe you are.

Prediction

You are in love with Florence
and the mystical body Christ,
you kneel at each altar
and pray for signs of His purity.

We stay outside the Roman gate
at the Classic Hotel on the road to Rome,
a fortune-teller lives in the garden,
you arrange to have your fortune told.

They serve breakfast in the cellar
with its murals of the holy land,
I go down alone
and sit at a rickety table
with a nun from Denmark.
She mentions
the residue of a stranger's soul
caught on the rim of a teacup
and then speaks only of angels and you,
she smiles when I tell her about
the little house in Calle San Sebastian
in the shadows of the ramparts
and predicts we will spend years
in Tuscany,
you as a silver olive tree
me as the wind in it.

Tathagata

The Buddha's wife speaks:
"When we first met,
orchards covered us,
luxuriant leaves
whispered precious secrets,
his eyes were my eyes.

When he felt our child stir inside me
he grew afraid,
his suffering damaged our love,
he named the boy Rahula, "Fetter" —
and disappeared in the night without a word.
his horse — Kanthaka — died of sorrow,
I had a son — death was not a way out for me.

Now they call him Arahant —The Blessed One,
Sage of the Republic of Sakka,
and that other name my heart knows better —
Tathagata —"Thus gone."

Autumn lovers

Afternoon's a rush of trees,
yellow wind unbraids the leaves
to sweep the naked shoulders of the hill.

Lovers lie together in the grass,
empty themselves into one another,
not in love but gratitude
that each is not the other.

Scent of stars

I cannot touch your body with its scent of stars,
I dream of more lives together than there are cherry petals,
Wake to find myself covered with touches and snow.

Corfu

At the beach at Paleokastritsa known for its unusual sunset

I turn my back on the sea,
in your eyes, I watch a dying sun slip below the horizon
yet it shines back through salt water

What we had — I squandered among dark men
clustered around tables gossiping and throwing dice,
I have trouble with boundaries,
where do we stop and other worlds begin?

Exhausted by the torments of love
your body rests against pillows of sand,
twilight thickens in the blood,
the coils of your hair bind up darkening heaven,
this naming of things has become so very silly,
a star is not a star

Anniversary

The gift I wanted to give you
these many years
was a beautiful life,
your smiles tells me
there is only one step left
to make my own life beautiful.

III

GO PALE INTO KANSAS

The memory is no friend.
It can only tell you
what you no longer have:

— Margaret Atwood,
from "The visit"

There's a certain slant of light,
Winter Afternoons —
That oppresses, like the
Heft of Cathedral Tunes —

— Emily Dickinson

listen to me as one listens to the rain,
the years go by, the moments return,
do you hear the footsteps in the next room?
not here, not there: you hear them

— Octavia Paz

Painters

> There is something bigger than fact: the underlying spirit, all it stands for, the mood, the vastness, the wildness.
>
> —Emily Carr

> I decided that if I could paint that flower in a huge scale, you could not ignore its beauty.
>
> —Georgia O'Keeffe

> I paint myself because I am so often alone and because I am the subject I know best.
>
> —Frida Kahlo

Emily Georgia Frida
sisters in paint and pain —
tree flower face —
transcended

Night Magic, Nuit Magique

A bar in old Montreal once frequented by L.C.

Night Magic's a mystery
A lion at the door
eyes in every shadow
gaze at lovers on the floor

The coat check girl is putting out
and smoking cigarettes
the bartender is mixing drinks
of bourbon and regret

The singer says you'll find him
by the exit at the back
he'll be reading Tarot cards
and drinking Johnny Black

He opens up a silver case
and offers you a smoke
he tells you that you're beautiful
you take it as a joke

He whispers by the fireside
that he's a creature cursed
the waiter is a Minotaur
the waitress is a nurse

He then draws up the Devil card
speaks softly of desire
and the heavy chains of longing
that the bonds of love require

That's when that you start to notice

the storm clouds in his eyes
and you think if you get close to him
you'll unmask his disguise

He says he'll never love you
he's not that kind of man
and as he bends to kiss you
the DJ plays *Suzanne*.

His house is old and tiny
in a careful *cul de sac*
the bed is cold and narrow
but you hold nothing back

Morning light
erases night
the mystery is gone
and all that you are left with
is this ghostly tarnished song.

Poetry class

Irving Layton
gray-mane lion
prophet-voiced
reads poems so soft and strong
images rise over earth
explode in storm and light

The *Gazette* calls one student's work
of love gone cold
mere "nutty mumbling"
Layton turns to the offending line
and reads:
"the sky fills up with cumulous regret"
we feel our neck hairs rise

January thaw

Heart of winter
my friend's wife has left him
he feels dead he says,
has two tickets for Cancun
will I fly down with him instead?

Air Canada out of Pierre Trudeau
I read Roberto Bolaño's
Savage Detectives
he drinks tequila straight.

At the beach
a sullen sea,
he won't leave the room,
she won't pick up his calls.
He goes downstairs
and throws his cellphone in the sea,
I suggest Mérida and he agrees.

Ancient purple bus,
seats in plush velvet,
plunges through night jungle,

Young Latino poets burn
For perfect poems
For perfect girls
Derelict big city spell
Criminals and whores
Fetid blooms — dank smells —
Evil perfume

Under the fleeting jungle floor
a million Mayans
permanently rest.

Outside a harsh-lit terminal
"Holiday Inn" he shouts —
"We're on holiday, holidaaaaaay."
Families doze in hammocks
hung in lighted rooms,
stray dogs, mansions in bad repair,
big leafy trees, the heat,
"*Si, we have rooms, señors*"

Late morning at Café Negro across the street
bitter espressos antidote for bitter dreams he says
unfaithful angel with a lonely voice he says
he's ruined he says and wants
to climb the ruins in his head,
we rent a car,
take the road south to Uxmal.

We stare up at the Pyramid of the Magicians,
No Trespassing,
Our eyes trace stone-faced rain god Chac into clouds,
bad weather coming
Footballs fashioned out of severed heads?
Jaguars still haunt the nunnery?
Why again did shamans eat those human hearts?

Stones carved with stories
pave the jungle underground
none to remember, none to care.

Rain blurs the sky
he's quiet now,
truth is he says
she left me for God.

Reasons to love America

Union Square,
Broadway and 4th Avenue,
cold pink April Saturday early,
Greenmarket setting up,

Last fall's apples in pine crates
March maple syrup
carted down from North Bennington
in back of a F-150 pickup,
1200 cans at $17.50 a throw,
worth getting onto I-87 South
by 3:30 am.

Walt Whitman pisses behind
Washington's big horse,
Ginsberg hunches around the corner,
heads down 21st Street for bagels,
passes a bundled Buddhist going east.

Henry Miller comes up
out of the 14th Street subway,
a smile on his face, not a sous in his pocket,
he's missed the poets, saints and soldiers,
but what can it matter, "*don't you see?*"

Across the street at Harlow's Diner
what remains of the dark sips black coffee,
the legs of the night waitress
go on pale into Kansas.

Kerouac

Driving half-awake
Cold coyote howl-dawn
High desert Arizona
I-40 semis swerving
Midnight truckers
Smoked-out reveries
Plump sleek sexy Jenny-Lou
Asleep back home in Tennessee
And me with Kerouac on CD
Dreaming down old meteor crater,
Hopi cloud-corn-clown,
Petrified forest, ghost buffalo
America New World Promise Paradise
So sweet, so broke

O Jack O Jack O
Beatific Bodhisattva wise-angel face
Haikus pouring off like milk
White light inner delight sphere music
Blessing form, inside torn
Froggy-Frenchy old Lowell Mass
Old Quebec wolf river
God visioned catholic loving
Soul
O Jack O Jack O

Frisco worn down dirty bar bash
Dipsy tipsy
Night hammer punch-out
Black silk-wet street shroud
Slouch-hat brown-bagged men

Nightmaring under Bowery-busted bridges
Train sound music
BOP, DE-BOP, BOP, DE, REBOP, DE-BOP

O Jack,
Dream shaper, pied piper piss-up
Heart-America prisoner-guard
Queer-twisted, planed down, blown-up,
Hope-koan Zen-land
Drunken asshole
Sublime, word-wringer, worry-warrior
Your songs, Jack
Jesus Jack, heart go pitter-pat
How you do that, Jack?
Who are we, Jack?
And who the hell are you, Jack?

Why you go down dead?
Why you go down dead, you bastard?
Why you leave us hummin', singin', screamin', joy-seekin'?
Why you put heaven in age-beaten, pee-pee pant,
Life-drifted street face?
Why you go down dead, Jack?
What we do from now 'til we,
You know, Jack,
'Til we
go
down dead
like you,
Jack?

Directions

Big white paddlewheel showboat
leans into tired telephone pole pier
Moline, sister turned to whoring,
skips pocket change on Mississippi scum,
Peeling double-wides and hell-hole bars
shunt strangers
down one-way Main Street where
a maze of side roads
locks you in,
night coming on,
ragged men with brown bag bottles
coming out,
America failure-fear
swallows open Prairie freedom.

Service station package-store guy
offers he sells more booze than gas
"Where you from?
"not from round here, I'd guess."
laugh turns to cough
"no way outta here
been trying for forty years
can't be done."
scratches his head and adds,
"unless you're a rich bastard,
used to screwin' everybody,
if you are, take a left at the next light
and floor the motha."

Back in the car
radio blaring
Woody Guthrie
"This land is your land,
This land is my land...
But not if ya don't got the
Dough, ray, mi..."

Escape!
sailing thru green night,
Santee Sioux country,
Kingdom of *Ohiyesa,*
child of earth embryo,
great-grandfather Sun
of lightning wind water fire frost,
knower of nature's abiding gifts,
writer of books
under that other name he took,
Charles Eastman,
explainer of Indian ways,
container of "mysterious feeling"
hambeday,
homage to you
Ohiyesa
your spirit moves against dark hills
star shadows honor you.

Long steamer rolls away south,
honky-tonk dance music,
orange moon drum beats,
singer wolf sits up,
howls for ice cream.

Equinox

Chile: Neruda in autumn

Fog fingers at a furious landscape
tremulous surf knits a ragged sweater of seaweed,
the ocean has nothing left to return,
sand shadows haunt the foam-fumed rocks,
I loved her — sometimes she loved me
River rain washes the salt wounds of the sea
She loved me — sometimes I loved her

The cranky house,
stuffed with old trophies that need a good dusting
sobs softly against the thigh of the hill,
fat autumn grapes jewel the sea-arbor,
plump, moist, sugared by summer,
sweet kisses in the hands of aging leaves
Ojo del Rey, they call them,
My grape eyes,
her almond eyes in an almond face,
I trust the roil of the sea
to sew up the tearing of a vacant heart —
this sweater still smells of her after 30 years.

Spain: Lorca in spring

Look! The anemone throws back her pink shutters,
she calls to her faraway cousins in the far sea,
Grape hyacinths peacock-preeners,
come, you too, worthy poppy,
tell me a story of life in the earth
you are proof of happy endings.
The violet wings of the archangel quiver
against the eyelids of new grass
the river warms its long tail in the sun.

Pretty green stamens — write your two cents' worth
on the clean white sky,
the wind is impatient to rush them
to Neruda,
he needs you

Poets' holiday

Neruda and Lorca Greyhound into Arizona
on a busman's holiday,
Pablo sports a cap with a poem embroidered inside,
Federico outfits himself with a straw Stetson from the gift shop,
The first night in the desert,
dozing under their hats,
they dream each other's dream
bees and lilies,
a woman and an ocean blanket them

Lorca moons over an orange-yellow poppy:
"They will come and cut off your head, my pretty,
Your green limbs desecrated under dark hooves.
The songs of praise I compose to your martyrdom
May be sung in splendid cathedrals
But what good will that do you?"

At the capital,
Neruda meets with a delegation of senators
And speaks his mind,
"Call me an undiplomatic, diplomat,
Bullets frame what you call freedom,
My friend Salvador walked to his death,
through a gateway marked "Democracy."
After the soldiers had violated what I held dear
not even a winter moon and the long white ocean
could restore the pure life I shared with my wife."

Next an ear of corn in the high country
teaches them to do the hokey-pokey
while beans and squash keep time,
Federico falls in love with a red cliff
and takes her to bed with him for a magic night,
Pablo sings sea shanties to a rushing river,
in answer to questions about flash floods
he uses a desert lake and the Pacific
to explain the nature of death.

Poets, corn, beans, squash and *rio* agree that stars conceal
the same secrets the whole universe over,
as they sail off in the cisterns of a sky the color of blood opals
to visit Octavio Paz in Mexico City.

IV

GUARDIAN OF CHILDREN, MAKER OF MUSIC

In Spain, the dead are more alive than the dead
of any other country in the world.

— Federico Garcia Lorca

I know a number of American and English males, working at
the fringes of journalism and literature, who systematically destroyed
their livers by sitting for years at...(the) sturdy tables (of Madrid's
Cerveceria Alemana) downing Fundador brandies and talking
Hemingway-tough about bulls and women.

— James Markham

Guardia Civil

A white town in Andalusia
strung along the mountainside like teeth,
teeth that bite.

Every day at 5:30 pm precisely
the captain and his sergeant
emerge from a shadowed doorway
armed with AK-47s,
stroll down the long lip of a street
from one end of the grin
beginning at their station
to the other
end at the church.

They do not smile.

Halfway back they enter a crowded bar,
bring silence with them like a dead hand,
Esteban, the owner, pours out two half-tumblers
of *Ciento Tres* brandy,
not the best,
not the worst.
the soldiers sip their drinks.
not too slow,
not too fast,
if there was a clock you could hear it tick
there is no clock,
only the sound of the town holding its breath
until these two spiders
scuttle under their noses
and are gone.

Bullfight

Low day whines in a grey wind,
a cadre of clouds taunts the church until
its sharp cross prods them
toward purgatory.

The town still stinks of the Inquisition,
even the crows have a pinched look,
bird bishops caught in their lies,
self-righteous still,
suspicious now
of any signs that claim to point to heaven.

I've come up from the coast
to see my first bullfight
drawn by a flamboyant poster
of a splashy matador
arched over horns and massive head,
and a terrible curiosity,

The bullring's square,
no bigger than a volleyball court,
The stands are boards
laid across stacked barrels,
a half-crazy dwarf hawks peanuts
to a wary crowd.

Wheezy trumpet fanfare
dies a rattling death in the far hills,
the fight begins.

Pale Miguel, not yet 16, enters
wearing a tight black homemade suit,

pride and uncertainty plainly at war within,
the bull, sleek and confident as a young Jesuit,
has no such doubts
and thunders forward
with a triumphant snort,
the boy stumbles and falls,
el toro passes over him like the apocalypse,
looks back with marble eyes,
paws at the sand.

The crowd holds its breath,
the young lad staggers to his feet,
Praise be to the blessed Virgin, he's alive
His mother rushes in,
sweeps him from the ring
cowled in her dusty shawl,
the bull takes a victory pass
smashes at the boards with bright horns,

The ticket holders stamp their feet and boo
two banderilleros try
to sink their ribboned barbs
between the beast's shoulders,
it looks like suicide,
in three attempts
not a single dart
touches the heaving flesh.

At length the featured matador appears,
a jittery old man poured into a faded suit of lights,
he struts, flings out his cape,
arches his back and struts again,
the bull throws him one unrepentant glance,
comes on like the Book of Revelations once again,

tears at the old man,
opens a gash below the knee,
the matador sags to the sand,
curls into fetal position,
draws his cape over his head,
trembling, the banderilleros return
to drag him from the edge of hell.

The cat-calling crowd now rises to its feet as one,
chanting "Money back! Money back!"
the promoter appears,
a fat man in a rumpled suit,
announces free drinks
at the town's only bar,
a thin rain begins to fall.

The bull shunts around the ring
like a runaway locomotive,
the butcher, in a bloody leather apron,
arrives armed with a large chisel and a club
after much waving of hands
the breeder punches his wallet pocket
and it's done,
weapons are put away.
No death this afternoon.

They toss the victor
two large of flukes of hay
and repair to the bar,
where wine flows like blood.

Fragrance of an idea

The perfume of an idea hangs in the air all afternoon,
we go over the wall of the Alhambra at midnight,
A thin sliver of a silver moon
coaxes luminous roses
to just hold their color in the pale night,
spicy air presses down on spilling pools,
filled with the same stars
the old kingdom wept under
and lost.

We brim with a catching beauty —
for all we imagine we are —
and may not become.

Seville Cathedral, 1506

Down the Guadalquivir sail the conquerors,
back comes gold suffused with blood and piety,
up goes the largest church in Christendom,
spired by Almohad's tallest minaret,
graced by the world richest altarpiece,
O Divine Joy,
O Supernal Light,
O Transcendental Bliss,
these are our gifts to your glory
yet — though we pray at your altar
'til our knees bleed —
you are silent.

Seville Cathedral, 2010

Ten a.m bells ring in the *Patio de los Naranjos*
amid dark leaves, the gleam of oranges
buzz of hornet, whisper of leaf,
sunshine pours out of Africa,
languid lovers lean to one another.

Inside the cathedral, light dim as a crypt's,
tourists and penitents cower in the transepts
stalked by the blazing eyes of a jaguar —
hungry stowaway from the new world,
they pray for the days when they were children
and faith was guardian and maker of music.

New Spain

Near Acoma
a massive outcrop
bursts the tawny skin of curving hills —
a jagged wound that will not ever heal.

Oñate and his conquistadors
come this weary way to war,
Cut off men's feet,
Rape,
March children into slavery,
Kill,

Earth remembers.

Writers in pain

We spend the winter on murky mountain
you in your small house and I in mine,
Spring comes, the rains stop,
we ride a rickety bus down to the beach,
we are poor and ragged with winter,
we strip down to our underwear
spread out on a shabby towel
and try to read,
you Shakespeare, I Cervantes.

It isn't quite beach weather yet,
pale Scandinavian girls,
still slog through the slush in Sweden,
German girls shiver in Munich,
London girls linger over pints
in chilly pubs.

At noon the sea has a grey and flaccid look,
a vicious wind licks at the sand,
we eat gritty tuna and tomato sandwiches,
and repair to an empty beachside bar
to wonder if we'll ever get laid again.

V

NOTHING STAYS THE SAME

The butterfly counts not months but
moments, and has time enough.

— Rabindranath Tagore

The only way to make sense out of change is to plunge
into it, move with it, and join the dance.

— Alan Wilson Watts

Knowing

Some nights when I was very young
I'd float up to the corner of my room,
look down to see myself lying in bed
and imagine I was dead.

The air smelled of sex,
and angels
and I knew for certain
earth was where
I was supposed to be.

Butterflies

My grandmother wore a necklace of jet beads
rainbows floating in them,
kept a small picture by her bed of the *Queen Mary*
floating on an iridescent sea,
told me the sky and ocean
were made of butterfly wings,
and made me cry,
butterfly wings belonged on butterflies,
nothing could be gained
by growing up.

Safe

Great Aunt Lula keeps a dozen chickens,
a pig and two sides of venison in a freezer
in the long loose-planked shed back of her kitchen,
the shed smells of wood smoke, donuts and sweet bacon,
my father — her favorite nephew — teases
it's more than she and Uncle Henry
could ever eat,
Uncle Henry stays in bed and eats cigars,
the doctor won't let him smoke

They send me out to play
behind the house
on the hill quilted with daisies,
a day mirror of night's dark ocean
sewn with random stars,
grasshoppers, mouths of green/brown spittle
beat against cupped hands,
ants work at their perfect architecture,
a star-nosed mole scuttles
with startled garnet eyes,
disappears.
Mother calls me in for lunch.

I'm sent to the cellar to fetch a jar of watermelon pickles,
standing in the dim drift of light and summer air
that filters through one small window laced with grass
I hear footsteps and muffled voices upstairs
and feel so safe I never want to leave.

Nothing stays the same.

My dog chased nuns

My dog Mittens
chased nuns,
He snapped at their skirts,
tore their habits,
My mother — good protestant woman —
but no seamstress —
kneeled on the sidewalk
and stitched up the ragged hems.
She pricked her finger
and whispered "*Damn it to Hell*"
under her breath.

Cars

In 1954 — the year my father turned forty —
he bought a 1948 Studebaker.
on his birthday morning
and every morning for a month after it
he half-sang in his loud, flat voice
Forty years ago a little babe was born and that was me

Forty seemed ancient to me
I feared he might be close to death
so I was cheered by the Studebaker,
green and modern as a rocket
that seemed to go
forward and backward at the same time,
This was no old man's car
my friends envied me for it

When it finally wouldn't start
he put it up on cinder blocks
and sat in it after dinner
two or three nights a week
and smoked a cigarette.

On a night
after his first heart attack,
he said to me "Judas Priest, son,
how I did love that Studebaker."

Wooden matches

Clearing out the house
after my parents died
I found a round ceramic doodad
about the size of a baseball,
family crest on the side,
two lions rampant,
top hollowed out to hold wooden matches.

I only ever saw my grandfather use it once,
I was four,
after a Sunday dinner at Grannie's,
Grandpa accepted a Pall Mall from my father,
and with some care,
selected a blue-topped, red-tipped wooden match
And struck it on the bottom.

A missionary, cheerful, very old,
And holy.

The war had ended,
I sat at the formal dinning table
on a parchment book
more than a foot high,
he'd brought back from India or Turkey,
before my mother was born,
Grannie gave it away
the day after he died.

Graves

I visit my parents' graves,
once a year in May, not more,
and think of them
as they are in photographs
taken before they married.

My mother — so often her own enemy —
leans against my father in his seersucker suit,
he smokes a cigarette — looks at home in the world.

I want to believe the dead
care about such visits
as my father always said they did
but something in me knows they don't.

Gift

You insisted on buying me this sweater
at the Buffalo Exchange.
That was ten years ago
on a brilliant October day
in Flagstaff's thin bright air,
when all that was important
was kindness.

VI

FORESTS OF THE HEART

Some people go to priests; others to poetry;
I to my friends.

— Virginia Wolf

Until one has loved an animal a part of one's
soul remains unawakened.

— Anatole France

Breakfast with Søren

Søren Kierkegaard had breakfast at IKEA the other morning,
he sat at a table in that tall black hat
Hans Christian Anderson had found so amusing,
his face, clean and kind, shone above
a cup of black coffee

I hesitated as I went by with my tray
and with a nod he invited me to sit,
I asked what brought him out so early,
he replied simply that he was an early riser
and offered he was there to buy a wooden chair

I pulled out my long shopping list,
In a voice soft and green as a leaf
he suggested I pare it down to just one thing,
his hand trembled a little as he raised his cup
but it was really nothing

After a silence
he rose.
a long-legged crane
rising from the edge of a river,
bowed ever so slightly,
wished me good day
and moved off
toward home furnishings,
a tall bright-eyed bird
crossing a sunlit clearing
in the forest of the heart.

Library transaction

Man with a worn tread face
clomps in with his possessions
tied up in two torn knapsacks
and a dark green garbage bag,
he's quiet, shy.

His big broken-tooth mouth,
red and wet with smiles,
terrifies.
He travels where we fear we too might go,
We struggle with it but we can't forgive.

I pass him a dollar folded in a book,
we do not speak,
neither is satisfied.

Via Rail, first class

Tall young mother
sleek, polished,
in her informal way,
jaunty white pedal-pushers
just cover her expensive knees,
bare cared-for feet
support her elegance quite perfectly.

She bends to adjust
the ear buds of her
second-youngest son,
good-looking boy

Money has made her even lovelier
than she is,
and makes me grateful
wealth can be used so well.

Concert

I fidget while the strings tune up,
brass and percussionists sit passively,
the conductor takes the stage, uncomfortable
in a role in which it's impossible to be modest,
arms raised,
a heartbeat of silence.

The sudden surge, a single soaring voice
silences this world, sweeps into that grand
chamber that abides in every heart.

Montreal candles

I go to Notre Dame
to light a candle
for a man who was a father to a friend,
the church hosts few worshippers,
since the quiet revolution
the faithful have mostly given up the faith,
the bishop has turned from collection plates
to public offerings of "*son et lumiere*"

I feel awkward kneeling at the empty altar
yet stilled and blessed too

The nave is cool and silent as the Sinai
forty days and forty nights spent on these
rough limestone tiles in prayer and contemplation
and you'd see God and touch his flesh

Venice in winter

A crescent moon lies in a manger of clouds,
cold and distant bells ring in sharp air.

Plaza San Marco is empty at midnight,
only a few pigeons rise toward heaven tonight,
frosty lamplight gilds their small angelic wings,
three magnificent cats from Florian's attend.

Fear of light and dark

Out of the dark woods
a borzoi of heart-stopping speed
streams across the long green pasture,
rushes into the cool house through the open terrace doors,
drops to the intricate carpet, panting,
gaping smile, lolling tongue,
her wolf teeth gleam.
What of those flecks of blood?
And is there evil in the world?
The rabbit makes no judgment,
The dog is at home in herself,
I am pursued by doubts,
torn by beauty and violence.

My dog dying

Daria, the swift, who smiles,
who will live forever,
is sick.
She lies on the cool tiles all day,
waits for evening,
too exhausted to chase rabbits
even in her dreams.
She may have diabetes,
She may have eaten poison meat,
Life may not be what we think it is
or death either.

Long wake

Five rushing days of wind in April,
the buds hold in their color tight,
juniper and pine sigh and groan,
moan at midnight in this
their season of purgatory.

Your mother died on Saturday,
her breath suspended,
her heart a buried bulb
that will not flower on earth again.
We store her ashes with your father's
in the column of a sundial in the back garden
and imagine her still taking tea
among the arrested roses.

The sun sweeps through the sky,
torn faces of scudding clouds
dissolving smiles, tears,
hours spill accelerated shadows 'round the dial.
You whisper of the struggle to forgive her — and yourself,
About how cold you feel and breathless
as though something entirely new is about to begin.

Last drink

I've been drinking all night,
in the dazzling dawn
a dog saunters up
and pees in the gutter

I have been here many times before,
my eyes blurred to a beauty I couldn't face
in myself or in the world

It's written
God spoke to Saul on that Damascus road
and struck him blind
then let him see again as Paul

I hear silence,
my vision clear,
the world pristine,
I can sing again.

Prairie meditation

After meditation class
a boy from St Boniface
asks — over beet soup
at Basil's on Osborne —
how to save his life.
He prays, struggles,
kneels by his bed,
by the altar, lights candles,
begs God to move in his heart.
Nothing,
no voice,
no special feeling,
he grows desperate

When knowing abandons us what remains
but an unsayable aloneness?
yet we go on as we have,
a twisted tree in an ocean of prairie,
until that awful solitude loosens,
as though for no reason,
and we find the thread again

Hiking heart mountain

O those mountains of the heart,
what journeys are taken there,
the way's both hard and easy,
Monday go alone singing,
Tuesday take love and water,
Wednesday, bread and patience,
Thursday pack fruit and harmony,
Friday peace and silence will suffice,
weekends are crowded,
bundle up all you can carry
and give it away.

Acknowledgements

I'm grateful to ever-vigilant editor Clarise Foster; many of these poems are tighter and more direct thanks to her attentive work.

Special appreciation goes to friends and readers, including those who know me better as Portlin Cochise, the late Torben Schioler and Christopher Lane, Maybin Esler, Robert Troutbeck, Carol Haralson, Robert Anderson, James Bishop, Jr, John Reid, Christopher Fox Graham, Suzanne Copeland, Mary Heybourne, Jill Williams, Jim Simmerman, and all others who have shared their good words.

I owe a lasting gratitude to my loving and supportive family for their patience and encouragement — first and foremost, my wife Valmai Howe and my daughter Tilke whose unerring ability to spot a line that doesn't quite work has been invaluable. Jonathan, Madeleine, Parker, thank you and love to you all.

About the Author

David Elkins is a poet and short-story writer. His work includes *A Bulldog's Guide to Small Engine Repair* (under the pseudonym Portlin Cochise) and *Relative Exposures: Felling the Family Tree* (co-written with Torben Schioler). His poems have appeared in numerous publications, including *Harper's Magazine, Panorama, Our Times,* and *Now*. He has won the International CKG Award for Poetry and was a finalist for QWF's A.M. Klein Award.

By way of keeping the wolf away from the door, Elkins has run rooming houses, made candles, worked as a waiter in honky-tonks, been a journalist and columnist for the *Financial Times of Canada*, built adobe and straw bale houses and launched a medical media company. He's run eighteen marathons and has meditated pretty much daily for the last thirty years. With the possible exception of meditation, he views these pursuits as a distraction from poetry. Things he values most: the love he shares with his wife Valmai, dogs, and people who are kind. These days he divides his time between Montreal and Santa Fe, New Mexico.

Eco-Audit

Printing this book using Rolland Opaque 50 instead of virgin fibres paper saved the following resources:

Trees	Solid Waste	Water	Air Emissions
1	61 kg	2,008 L	187 kg